St. Davids

(Tŷ ~~Ddewi~~)

the **City** ... wi

GW00706100

and the **Coa**

by **Tony Roberts**

Sketch Maps and Illustrations by
Elizabeth Roberts

Abercastle Publications

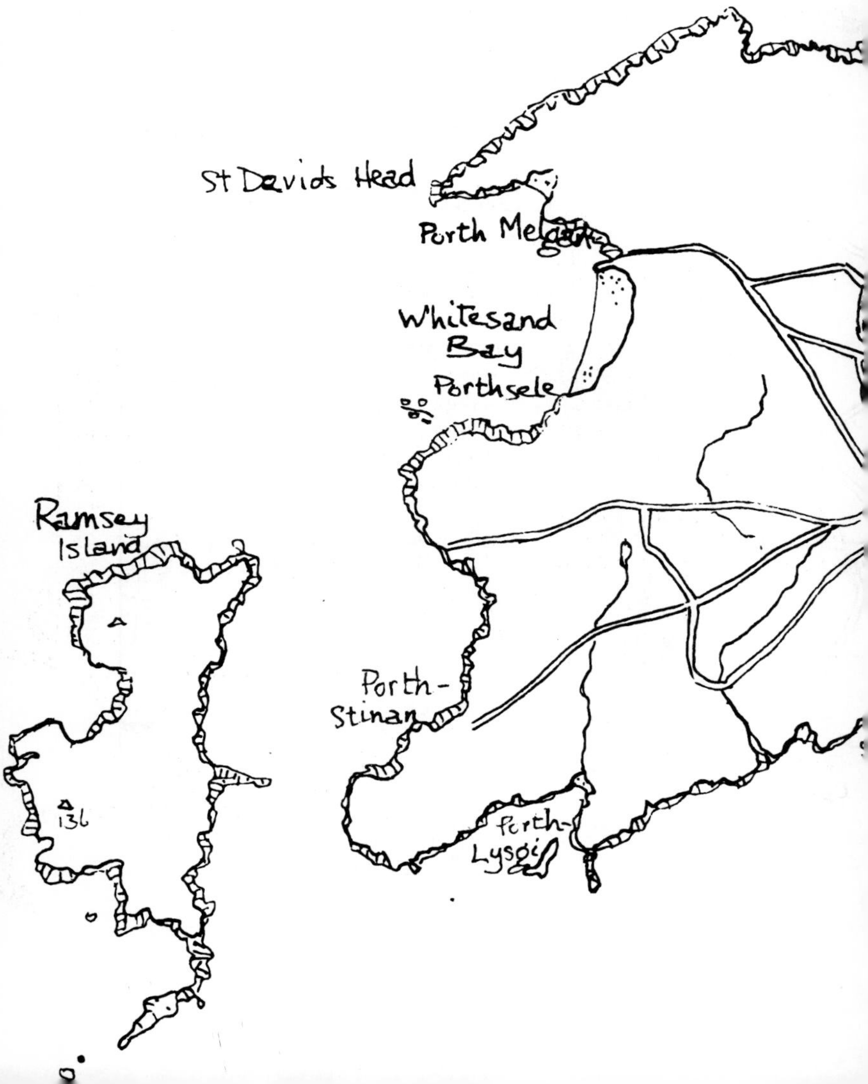

St Davids Head

Porth Melgan

Whitesand Bay

Porthsele

Ramsey Island

Porth-Stinan

Porth-Lysgi

136

Contents

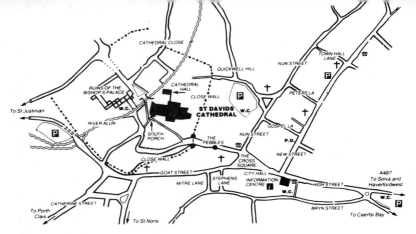

A Walk through the City and Cathedral

If you are in St. Davids for one day, you need a system of priorities to get the most out of it. Of course, you can't do justice to it in a short time, but sometimes circumstances dictate.

Anyway, first get the feel of the place, but don't take long over it. St. Davids is no aesthetic jewel: most of the buildings are standard early 19 Century vernacular, to put it kindly. So, take one half-day to look round the town, quickly, and do the Cathedral; and the other half-day to walk to the nearest coast which is St. Non's Bay, and there you will see a microcosm of the antiquities, and some fine coast-line.

Shopping may detain you a while: craft shops, woollens, books, souvenirs, there are some good things around quite apart from low-priced souvenirs.

Let's start with the Cathedral: and not only the Cathedral but the whole Close: the Bishop's Palace, the rural Close itself and the Cathedral. Start by the medieval cross.

Walk down the Pebbles, under the Tower and down the 39 Articles (the 39 steps) to the south porch. It is the setting which is unique, there is nothing like it in Britain, a majestic, but rural medieval scene, enhanced if the fine Welsh Black Cattle are grazing outside the Palace.

Car Parks are discreet; nothing like the monstrous visual affronts so many medieval sites have to suffer. If you don't fancy coming back up the steps, park down below. If you haven't too long, do the Bishop's Palace from the outside; the best things are the Rose Window tracery and the unifying arcading which are seen from the outside anyway; have a walk round and look through the Gatehouse.

Walk down past the Treasurer's house (inside is the seat St. Patrick sat on thinking about his job prospects in Ireland in the 5C).

Pleasant walk looking at a few of the houses in the Close, turn right and up Quickwell hill (several attractive cottages) and back into the town.

4

A Walk to the Coast and St. Non's Chapel

An easy half mile walk to the south is St. Non's Bay, along a pleasant lane out on to fields leading to the cliffs. Go down Goat Street, bear left at the plethora of signs and keep straight on, Warpool Court Hotel is on the right; and ahead you will see a large house – a Passionist retreat, where there is a tiny car park.

An enclosure in the field on the right contains St. Non's chapel and just before you get to it, on the left, is St. Non's Well. This spot comprises some of the basic religious mythology of Wales; with attractive coastal scenery. And in a short walk, some pleasant and unobtrusive wild flowers: gorse at any time – and the rest according to season.

Whether St. David was really born here is open to doubt. Hen Fynyw in Cardiganshire is also a claimant. But this is traditionally the place and pilgrims still came to St. Davids (two pilgrimages equalled one to Rome). From here, a typical cliff-top chapel, offerings were taken to the cathedral 'by the dishfull', until the Reformation, when the place fell into ruins.

St. David was born during a violent thunderstorm; it was round about 520 A.D. and a chapel was dedicated later. Beneath the altar was a stone said to bear the marks of his mother's fingers as she clutched at it during her labour.

The Well, a curing well for eye ailments and for wishing, was restored and re-dedicated by the Catholics. It may have been a holy well in pre-Christian times.

There is nothing to date the chapel. A chapel was mentioned here in a 14C document, and there is a pillar-stone with a simple Latin incised cross, which dates from 7 to 9C.

St. Brides Bay ahead, with the Marloes peninsula and Skomer on the sky-line.

Dewi Sant and his house (Tŷ Ddewi)

Most people coming for the first time are delighted to find St. Davids so small and unpretentious a city. (City is a courtesy title only, because of the Cathedral.) It makes no claims to beauty but at least it isn't some manicured Cotswold stockbroker film set.

In fact it is an agricultural village with the astonishing good luck to have Saint David (Dewi Sant) and a wonderful coast-line.

No railway ever came here: people still talk of the road from Haverfordwest '17 miles and 16 hills' which conjures up pictures of coaching days. It's a good road, not too spoiled or straightened, a tricky hill at Newgale, a bit of congestion at Solva but plenty of wild flowers.

The other road into St. Davids is from Fishguard, again pleasant enough but undistinguished. In both directions, the first view promises a dim little town with modern bungalows. The best approach is the east road from Abercastle, Trefin and Llanrian but it's best not to talk about it too loudly or they'll improve it.

The area is flat and treeless. On the coast just north of the town are the deceptive little peaks of Carn Llidi and Penberi, rocky hills which have resisted glacial erosion. It's all farming and tourism hereabouts: dairying, early potatoes and increasing numbers of sheep. And there is a small, but welcome tendency to organic agriculture. For the rest of it, caravans, guest-houses, a few hotels, self-catering and farm holidays. And increasing unemployment as the military establishments close down, and are replaced by committees, and Government crocodile tears.

Saint David started a community here in the 6C; it flourished and its founder became the foremost religious figure in Wales. A cathedral was built at a later date and an imposing Bishop's Palace. But of course there's much more to it than that. Why in such a remote place?

The answer is that it wasn't remote at that time. The early spread of Christianity in Celtic Britain centred to a large extent on this rugged coast, an inter-section of the sea-route from North-west Europe to Ireland.

The Christianity that reached these shores was different from that of our days. It was an ascetic, monastic Christianity owing most to a desert, eremitic tradition, and less to Rome. Much of our knowledge is speculative: its connection with territoriality and royal ancestry. For example: David is alleged to be descended from Cunedda, legendary king from Strathclyde who, brought by the departing Romans, expelled the Irish from north Wales and Dyfed. David was the son of Sant, king of Ceredigion. Did Dewi get a grant of land for his monastery? And whose was it to give – or did it 'belong' to an Irish overlord; the Deisi from south-east Ireland had invaded Dyfed and held it for an unknown period. Was the Boia story in Rhygyfarch's life of Dewi descriptive of the struggle between Irish and Welsh and between Christian and Druid. Or was it an attempt by the Welsh, Romanised and Christianised to expel their Irish colonial rulers?

Anyway Dewi himself, a most impressive figure, the Waterman who not only drank only water, but stood in it for long periods, *pour encourager les autres*, to use the phrase Voltaire used in a very different context thirteen hundred years later.

Dewi was dramatically successful. His influence spread; more than fifty churches were dedicated to him. His 'official' biography by Rhygyfarch employs all the official miracles etc., his journey to Jerusalem, his triumphant appearance at Llanddewi Brefi where by a miracle the ground rose beneath him so that everyone would hear him denounce a revival of Pelagianism, a seemingly very sensible heresy of Celtic origin and which the Church had particular difficulty in dealing with.

Perhaps the most impressive part of Rhygyfarch's biography is the description of life in the monastery: the rigour of work, in the fields, ploughing without oxen, the ascetic life, the caring life, the strictness and discipline. And, on the lighter side, the efforts of Boia and his wife to get rid of their new neighbour down to sending the handmaidens to do a striptease and use lewd gestures to destabilise the monks. Though that, and the ritual hairdressing and sacrifice of the daughter, were probably part of a Druidic ceremony to get rid of David.

Whatever 'cathedral' buildings there were, Vikings, probably from Dublin, destroyed several times; but then the Normans came.

The Marcher lords thrust in most parts of Wales, though not into St. Davids until William I himself came in 1081. It was not long before a Norman bishop was appointed. Though Bernard, who succeeded the Celt Wilfred became a staunch defender of the paramountcy of St. Davids. Two bishops later, de Leia started to build present cathedral. The Bishop's Palace began soon after. And Norman pomp had replaced Celtic simplicity. St. Davids became another See of the Church of England until 1921 when the church was disestablished.

The Cathedral and Close

St. Davids is rightly considered to be the glory of Wales. But not just the bricks and mortar of the Cathedral buildings, fine though they are. Indeed the Cathedral itself is modest compared with Salisbury or Lincoln, Exeter or Durham. True, none of these has anything to compare with the Bishop's Palace; and none of these has a rural close to compare, even though the houses in our close have fallen down and now date only from the 18C or 19C.

St. Davids still seems to have the inspiration of Dewi Sant himself, a tradition of fifteen hundred years of pilgrimage. His aura of simplicity and asceticism seem to pervade the atmosphere; the site was, after all, five hundred years old when William the Conqueror visited it.

In fact, what we see today would hardly have appealed to David and his chaps and the pomp of the medieval cathedral at its height with royal trains and pilgrims and their offerings all round, was out of key with his presence.

That stern and simple man who adjured his monks to withstand the wiles of Boia's wife's sirens would have been out of place in the 15C Palace.

Let's look at the Cathedral as we have it. It has been added to and restored so much that virtually every architectural period is contained within. The extraordinary thing is that all merge into a totality.

The outside is dignified rather than attractive but the interior is both light and rich. Building began in 1176; de Leia's nave and columns were late Norman, and very majestic they look, and it is transitional between Norman and Gothic.

The building was certainly not plain sailing; when one enters now, we see the floor sloping upwards and the columns leaning outwards; buttresses had to be added on the north side in the 15C to keep the wall up.

The Lady Chapel was added in the 13C and then in the 14C Bishop Gower took a masterful hand. He

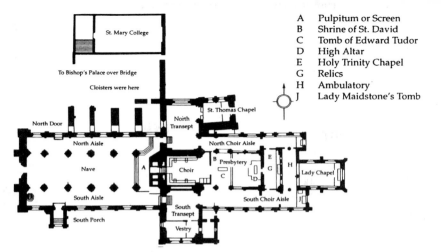

put in the huge screen the size of a small room with his own tomb taking up most of the space. He also put on the south porch. The aisle windows were re-done in the Decorated style of the period.

The splendidly ornamental oak ceiling was added to the nave by treasurer Pole about 1500, and the equally splendid Perpendicular ceiling put in the Holy Trinity Chapel by Bishop Vaughan in the 15C.

There were minor hiccups on the way: Nash re-did the West Window in the 18C and then the civilised Bishop Thirlwall had Sir G. G. Scott restore the tower, and remove Nash's work, replacing it by a reconstruction of the original.

There are lots of interesting things: more than one can cover in a page here. Here are some of the best: the beautiful Triple Lancet Windows in Early English style. Since Vaughan's chapel was the other side, they are useless for the purpose of light, and were filled in with mosaics.

Then there are St. David's and St. Justinian's relics, and the rather disappointing shrine; the tomb of Edmond Tudor, father of Henry VII. Then, in the south choir aisle is the tomb of the greatest of south Wales princes, Rhys ap Gruffydd and beyond Rhys's tomb is that of Giraldus Cambrensis, who fought so desperately for the independence of the Welsh clergy from the See of Canterbury.

Then, the fan-traceried roof of Vaughan's chapel. Perhaps one of the most interesting things is the misericords: those decidedly non-religious little carvings on the underneath side of the tip-up seats provided to relieve the tiredness of the elderly prelates in their long services.

The carvers were allowed free scope of choice of subject matter. There are a couple of interesting boat repairing scenes, one showing Gawain being sea-sick, several suggesting that the monks were no better than they ought to be: monkey figures suffering from the effects of over-eating and drinking.

The Close

The setting of the Close itself is often overlooked, so striking are the Cathedral and Palace.

The now ruined wall had four gates, of which only one is left. This is Porth y Twr, coming from the square and leading down the road past the Deanery to the Cathedral. It is built against the bell tower, 13C. It originally enclosed the city itself.

The view is spectacular: the Cathedral and Palace, the little river dividing them, the trees and rooks, the dignified, if not distinguished 18/19C houses where once the canons lived.

It was the early bishops, men like Bek and Martin, and above all de Gower, who were the builders. Men of power, close to the King, who brought energy and ability and by 1350 had changed the early medieval site of St. David into something sumptuous. True, there was still the other Tudor work of Bishop Vaughan to come, but the Close wall was there before 1200 for Henry II to be met at the gate.

There in the centre is the ford, where Dr. Middleton thinks David's monks were faced with the maidens of Boia's wife doing a medieval strip tease – 'concubitis simulant' – to destabilise them: and nearly succeeding.

And there is the bridge on the site of Llech Lavar, the talking stone, where Henry II met with a disputatious Welsh lady.

This is all in a remote and almost mythical past. But the rot set in early. After all, it was by 1200 that King Richard 1 reproved a monk who told him he (the King) would never find favour with God till he had married off his abominable daughters. The King replied that he had bequeathed his Pride to the Templars who were as proud as Lucifer, his Covetousness to the Cistercians, who covet the devil and all; and his Licentiousness to the Prelates of the Church who have the "most pleasure and felicitie therein" (Giraldus Cambrensis)

Who can wonder at the Reformation, at Bishop Barlow and the Dissolution?

The Bishop's Palace

This must be one of the most graceful ruins in Britain. It can hardly have looked more imposing when in full use. It grew up, more or less with the Cathedral, to receive pilgrims. To get to this remote corner must have been a formidable task for most pilgrims Two pilgrimages here equalled one to Rome; but this Palace doesn't seem particularly suited for ordinary pilgrims; this was rather for entertaining the well-heeled.

It was started in the 12C, added to in the 13C and finished off, as it were, in the episcopate of Henry de Gower (1327-48); to him is usually ascribed most of the credit for the building.

It is built round a court-yard and consists of a Great Hall, visible as you look in the gatehouse, and another hall at right-angles, which was the Bishop's Hall; with a Solar, then a couple of kitchens and a couple of chapels.

It is hard to say what the earliest part was (the north-west block) since only the undercroft vaulting is left.

But so skilfully did Gower decorate the parapet with chequer board arcading that the whole looks like a unified building.

There is a particularly fine wheel window in the Great Hall.

The Palace gains by being seen from the outside, it is both imposing and restful, while the bareness of the inside is a bit of anti-climax for most visitors.

Gower did in fact use the chequerboard arcading in Lamphey Palace and Swansea Castle as well.

Though there is a castle-like look about the whole building there is no suggestion of fortification or a portcullis in the entrance. And there was a motte and bailey castle, presumably by an early bishop, south-west of the city. Nobody seems to know – or care – much about it.

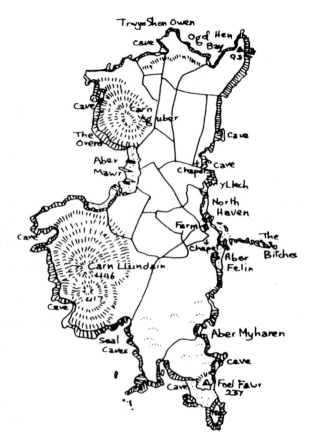

Trwyn Shon Owen

Cave

Ogof Hen Bay

93

Cave

Carn Ysguber

Cave

The Over

Aber Mawr

Chapel

Cave

y Llech

North Haven

Farm

Cave

Chapel

The Bitches

Aber Felin

Carn Llundain 446

217

Cave

Cave

Seal Caves

Aber Myharen

Cave

Cave

Foel Faur 237

Ramsey Island

What magic do islands have? Perhaps it is a longing for solitude and isolation. It can hardly, in Pembrokeshire, be the land and seascapes of the islands, for they can be equalled along the coast. But to experience peace and quiet, surrounded by sea, sometimes soothing, sometimes hostile, but always a shielding barrier; that is a dream we all cherish. Whatever it is about islands can easily be realised in Pembrokeshire.

There is Caldey Island and its monastery and crowds. St. Margarets, close by, in its solitude – no landings except for cormorants.

Then Skockholm, Skomer and Grassholm off the Marloes peninsula and finally Ramsey, by St. Davids. Trips to it, and round it, go every day from Easter to October.

Ramsey is a couple of miles long by a mile wide and some 600 acres in extent. It is hilly and rough land, a flat plateau with two heather-clad hills rising from the exposed and tree-less island; but it is farmable, though used now as a bird sanctuary. It is owned by the R.S.P.B. with manager and warden.

Ramsey Sound which separates the island from the mainland is treacherous and difficult, half-a-mile to a mile wide, with a dangerous tide, and a nasty ridge of rocks, the Bitches, at the narrowest part.

The Welsh name is Ynys Dewi or Ynys Dyfanog; there is also another Welsh name, Ynys yr Hyrddod, Island of the Ram.

The two hills, Carn Llundain and Carn Ysgubor, both have cairns on top (sepulchral?); there were on the island two chapels, one dedicated to St. Justinian and the other to St. Dyfanog. St. Justinian, a Breton, was St. David's confessor and he retired to Ramsey, so the legend goes, because of the lax ways of the mainland monks. Taking an axe, he cut the connecting land to the mainland but the axe becoming blunt left the Bitches; the last gap between Ramsey and the rocks is known as the Axe.

The other legend of Justinian was his decapitation. St. Dyfanog retired to Ramsey to end his days in peace.

For many centuries, the island belonged to the Bishops of St. Davids; and since medieval times, it was farmed and stocked with sheep and cattle. It was a productive farm, growing good corn as well as its stock and dairy products. It suffered in the same way as mainland farming, from Government neglect in many inter-war years; but transport and extra handling of everything threw an additional burden on tenants.

For the visitor, the island is a delight, though it lacks puffins and Manx shearwaters, since the presence of rats prevents any ground-nesting birds, unlike Skomer.

But Ramsey is far more exciting scenically than the other islands, with its high west face, wild inlets, bays and cliffs where the guillemots and razorbills breed, as well as fulmars, kittiwakes and buzzards. Moreover, Ramsey is the finest place to see seals. In the early autumn, the grey seals calve on the cave beaches in considerable numbers.

The landing quay on the island was built by making a wall from the island to the adjoining rock.

The round-the-island trip is best for seeing the seals and sea-birds but walking round Ramsey can be a magical experience, with the combined sea and solitude, wild flowers and birds. It takes about three or four hours to go right round the island but you can reach Carn Ysgubor in the north, in about half an hour.

At any time you may see buzzards, kestrels or a peregrine; ravens, choughs, crows and jackdaws; gulls: herring, great and lesser black backed; meadow pipits, lapwings and curlews. On sea and cliffs only guillemots and razorbills, fulmars, kittiwake gulls; shags and cormorants often on guard as you approach.

Details from Information Centres and notices in the square.

The Coast Path round the St. Davids Peninsula

Apart from seeing the Cathedral, the best thing around here is the scenery of the coast. And it can be walked on the Coast Path quite easily in sections.

If you can, drive or get driven to the Path; the roads leading up to it are not very interesting; though if you can't find a second driver, use the shortest route to the coast. Check on the sketch map.

Whitesands Bay to Caerfai is 8½ miles, about 3½ hours, quicker than most parts of the Path because the land is flat and the going is easy. You'll find you usually do about 2 miles an hour.

Shorter: **Whitesands to St. Justinians**: 2½ miles, just about an hour's walking. Parking.

St. Justianians to Porth Clais is just under 2 hours, about 4 miles.

Porth Clais to Caerfai is about two miles, just under an hour. Parking.

Finally, **Caerfai to Solva** is four miles, 2 hours. Again car parking either end.

The walking needs little description; it is level and good walking on springy turf, with fine wild flowers, especially in the spring, though I must say the wild look in the winter is rather fine.

The presence of Ramsey Island on the starboard side adds some variety to the scenery and the sight of St. Brides Bay is quite simply stunning, with Skomer at the southern end.

There are more grey seals round here than anywhere else you can find, and a wonderful range of birds, especially sea-birds. Auks – razor-bills and guillemots, gulls of all sorts. A very fine Iron Age castle, Castell Heinif a bit beyond St. Justinians, another, Penpleidiau, between Caerfai and Caerbwdy; and a third just past Porth-y-draw.

At Ogof y Ffos is the beginning of the strange Ffos y Mynach, originally a ditch which cut across the peninsula up to near Penberi, whose origin is still unknown. Plenty more historical oddities, whose very existence is underlined by the absence of later development, in fact not all that much since King Arthur came ashore at the port of St. Davids, after the huge Boar, Twrch Trwyth (see page 27).

In the other direction, **Whitesands to Abereiddi** is long and quite hard work. **Abereiddi to Porthgain** is a short walk finishing down at the harbour. Then from **Porthgain to Abercastle** is a nice easy walk.

Clegyr Boia near St. Davids

Map labels: N.T., Carnllidi, Carnedd Lleithr, Hut Circles, Coetanar thur (Cromlech), Crisal, Enclosures, Burial Chambers, Llaethdy Y.H.A., Trefelly, (camp), Porth, Maen Megan, Maen Siol, St Davids Head, Pwll Uog, St Patricks Chapel, Whitesand Bay or Porth-Mawr, Traeth-mawr, Car park, The Burrows or Tywyn, to St. Davids

Whitesands
and St. Davids Head

Whitesands, or Porth Mawr, is probably the favourite beach, and it has a both scenically and historically fascinating area next door. Large, with car park, shop, lavatories etc. Life guards too – northern end can be dangerous. St. Patrick's Chapel is just in from the car park.

St. Davids Head and Carn Llidi are an ideal half day's walk. You can make a nice couple of hours round walk, from the car park, up to St. Davids Head, over to Carn Llidi and back down footpaths.

A prehistoric roadway may well have gone down here on the way to Ireland. Men were active here five thousand years ago; this small area could well be a microcosm of the history of the peninsula. Between the actual headland and Carn Llidi are three neolithic burial chambers, not spectacular, but good enough. Further along you

can see outlines of some rare, remaining Iron Age fields, at least you can see the outlines when the bracken is low. Most striking of all is the actual headland. A large hundred yard ramp (the Warrior's Dyke, Clawdd y Milwyr) shuts off an eight or so acre site. Dates back two thousand or so years. There is a traceable entrance and the remnants of a couple of smaller stone walls. Excavated in 1890 and below the remains of half a dozen huts were found pottery sherds, beads and spindle whorls, etc. (in Tenby Museum). This was a defended fortlet which a small group could withdraw to.

There are places where you have to follow footpaths, but up on St. Davids Head and Carn Llidi, though paths are clear, it doesn't matter so much where you walk; keep out of boggy bits.

Whitesands Bay to Porth Clais

Almost as enjoyable in winter as in summer. The sea is no millpond, but it gains in grandeur.

Drive down to Whitesands, past the St. Davids golf links, much of the area dunes stabilised by marram grass.

Porthsele is the first beach south of Whitesands, adjoining at low water. Some fine old farmhouses – Rhosson, Treleddyn. Rhosson is one of the old 'round-chimneyed' houses and Treleddyn is where some two hundred years ago lived Capt. Williams who first identified the French 'invaders' of Fishguard.

Ramsey (Ynys Dewi) – all the islands have Norse names. Ramsey, separated by a usually fierce sound, lies just over half a mile off. Owned by the R.S.P.B. it is a Bird Sanctuary with fine colony of Grey Seals in the waters below.

St. Justinians (latinised version of Stinian) has some parking space. The Lifeboat is kept here. And trips for Ramsey depart. Parking; road access.

Castell Heinif is a fine double-banked promontory fort with a hundred yard long entrenchment cutting off a small promontory. Then there is an erstwhile copper mine which you pass. About a hundred and fifty years old, and never very successful.

More fine walking through heather, gorse and bracken till you round the corner and are going east, outside Treginnis Farm (N.T.).

Pass Porth Henllys and Porth Lysgi, diminutive and secluded beaches, then you come to Porth Clais.

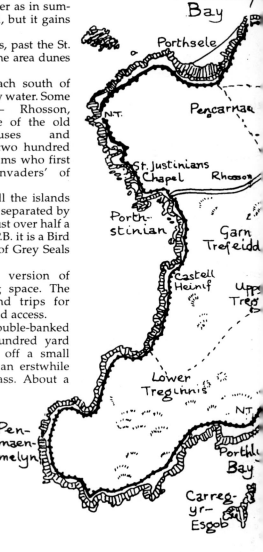

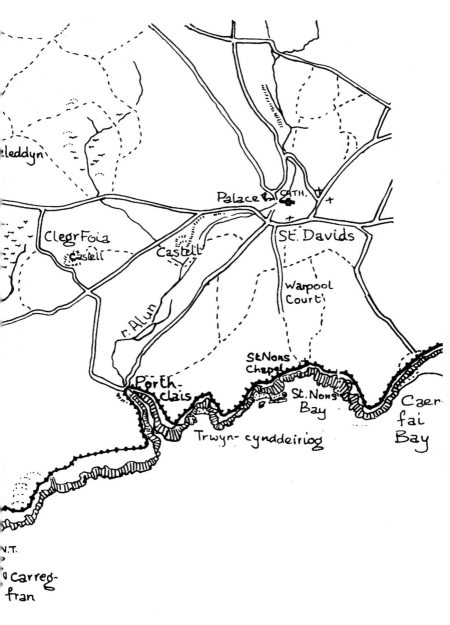

leddyn

Palace

CATH. †
+

ClegrFoia
Castell

Castell

St. Davids

Warpool
Court

r. Alun

St.Nons
Chapel

Porth-
clais

St.Nons
Bay

Trwyn-cynddeiriog

Caer
fai
Bay

N.T.

Carreg-
fran

Porth Clais to Caerbwdy

This is one of the most accessible stretches on the Coast Path. Close to St. Davids itself; and certainly the short stretch from Porth Clais to Caerfai has some beautiful scenery and an unequalled view across St. Brides Bay. (Map begins on P. 17).

Porth Clais was the port for St. Davids. As early as 1385 cargoes were brought in for the cathedral. In Elizabethan times, timber came from Ireland and corn, malt and wool went to Bristol and Barnstable.

The harbour wall has long been ruined and although coal was being brought here even after the war for the gasworks (now a car park), there wasn't much of a port after 1800. Small boats use the harbour now.

Twrch Trwyth, the fabulous boar with comb and scissors in his head, which King Arthur wanted, landed here from Ireland; more of the story on page 27.

St Non's bay is next, after rounding Trwyncynddeiriog, so-called Mad Point from the prevailing gales.

Make the short detour inland to see St. Nons chapel and also the well a few yards away. (See P. 5).

The large conspicuous grey building is a Passionist monastary.

The pillar stone has an incised ring-cross (left), a simple one, thought to be about 7th to 9th century, so it is unlikely to be anything to do with St. Non or St. David himself.

You can't go down to the beach here, but if you wait a bit till Caerfai, there is a fine accessible sandy beach below the car park.

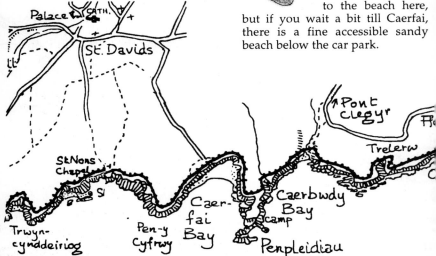

Caerbwdy to Solva

A very pleasant walk, quite short and easy. It is a little over two miles, but level mostly, so you can make good time, unless you choose a windy day and you are unlucky enough to have to walk into the wind. Same applies if you walk in the morning into a full sun.

You can drive most of the way down to Caerbwdy; turn off the St. Davids-Solva road at Pont Clegyr. As with Caerfai, some of the stone for Cathedral repairs comes from here. Fine square lime kiln. After some ¾ mile you come to a bit of a mystery: at Ogof y Ffos begins a strange 'way', ditch, bank or whatever: it begins here and threads its way across the peninsula, finishing up by Penberi. This Ffos y Mynach (Monk's Way) makes a good five mile walk (leaflet from Information Centre). Could have been an early medieval sanctuary border.

Cross over Morfa Common and you come to Porth y Rhaw, a glacial meltwater valley leading up to the road at Nine Wells. Fine big promontory fort, considerably eroded.

Solva is a long harbour which dries out quite a lot. Small pleasure vessels only, nowadays. The long headland has a promontory fort. They must have been a combative lot, the people who built their defended settlements every few miles along the coast about two milennia ago just before the Romans invaded Britain. Though it doesn't seem that even the biggest hill-forts held them up much. After all, it didn't take Vespasian long to knock over Maiden Castle.

Much of St. Davids' peninsula including this south coast and St. Davids head are National Trust owned. Being concerned with conservation they are encouraging traditional practices such as grazing and cutting bracken in an attempt to benefit wildlife.

If you want to walk more of the Coast Path, try it with our little Coast Path Guide which describes the whole of it.

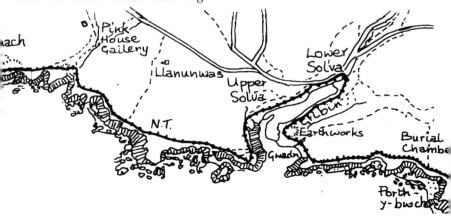

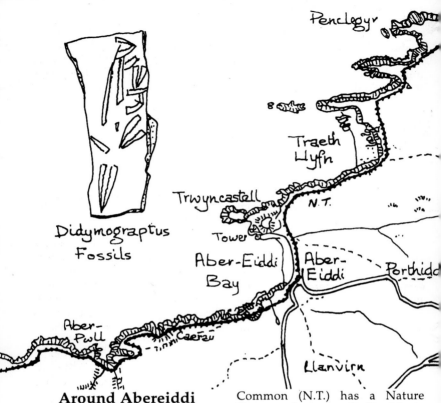

Didymograptus
Fossils

Penclegyr

Traeth
Llyfn

N.T.

Trwyncastell

Tower

Aber-Eiddi
Bay

Aber-
Eiddi

Porthidd

Aber-
Pwll

Caerau

Llanvirn

Around Abereiddi

There's a good five miles from Whitesands to Aberpwll, a majestic and impressive Coast. It's wild and craggy on the seaward side, well farmed on the landward. Harder walking than round the St. Davids Peninsula. Wild flowers equally impressive. I haven't put a map of this area in here because there's no car access.

Then, Aberpwll and Abereiddi a little under 2 miles. First, past Carn Llidi comes Carn Penberi; after this the land is lower, the farming better. Fine Iron Age forts at Caerau.

Further inland, Dowrog Common (N.T.) has a Nature Reserve along the St. Davids to Llanrian road, a few tiny hamlets – Rhodiad, Berea, Cwmwdig. At Rhodiad is Maen Dewi, a fine Bronze Age standing stone. The narrow Llanrian road is much pleasanter than the main road.

Abereiddi, sadly, is a village of holiday cottages, a fine bay, rocky and shingly with a large car park – good local walking. The Blue Lagoon, man made, was once a slate quarry.

The National Trust, who own the coast between here and Porthgain, are planning to preserve the industrial ruins.

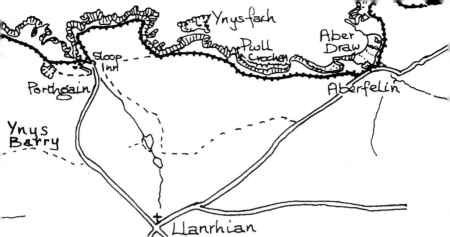

Porthgain

Porthgain formerly had quarrying and fishing. The small harbour (improved in 1902) exported crushed stone up to 1931. Despite a derelict air, the place is very alive, with a pub and a restaurant. But the stone workings are defunct and the crushers and bins empty. In the Spring of 1981, the houses were sold to local people and the National Park Authority bought the ruins and harbour. If you are interested in the history there is a booklet, 'About Porthgain', in this series.

Llanrhian is a hamlet ½ mile inland from Porthgain. Small, attractive church. Manor House farm buildings dominate what's left of the village; Trevacoon, a fine 18C farmhouse, is all that remains of another large estate. Village of Llanrhian has all but gone – school, shop, P.O. and mill.

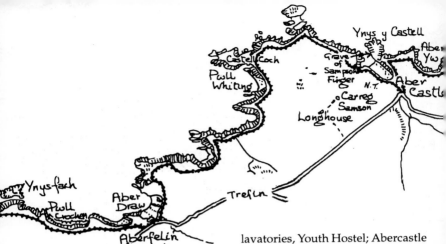

Abercastle

No apologies for concentrating here on the coast; it is more interesting than inland. It is all farming hereabouts: corn, early potatoes by the coast, dairying, sheep, beef, daffodils and tourism, though not obtrusively so.

Aberfelin is an attractive little bay. Scene of well-known Welsh poem by the archdruid Crwys, "The mill does not grind tonight at Trefin beside the sea ..."

It is claimed that a mermaid sat down by Aberfelin and the quarrymen heard her singing ... "reaping in Pembrokeshire, weeding in Carmarthenshire." Though, naturally she was singing in Welsh. Similarly, this was one of the places from which could be seen the "green islands of enchantment".

The coast all along here is of exceptional beauty: good walking, parking at Trefin, Abercastle. Trefin has various facilities: Pub, shop,

lavatories, Youth Hostel; Abercastle has only a lavatory and its own intrinsic attractiveness. Very limited car parking. Once a genuine small port, ships trading with Bristol, large ruined storage granary on coast path, dating from Tudor times. Very large modern bungalow conspicuously on the cliffs. On Longhouse, a large farm now owned by the National Trust, is a very fine Neolithic burial chamber called Carreg Samson. Reached from either the Coast Path or from the road, just a field from the farm. Just drive down, but don't park outside farm gates. A 300 BC. Iron Age promontory fort, Castell Coch, is situated between Trefin and Abercastle.

At Longhouse Farm, too, in 1743, Howell Davies 'the Apostle of Pembrokeshire', Howel Harris and Daniel Rowlands, three of those most intimately connected with the Non-Conformist movement in Wales, met. The preaching of these pioneers attracted huge audiences.

Lime Kilns, Holy Wells, Chapels

The St. Davids area hides a splendid variety of interesting subjects, three of which we are outlining here.

Lime Kilns

The round lime kilns which are to be found alongside small harbours, occasionally on open beaches, are a fascinating relic of the agricultural past.

Limestone, crushed or broken up, was burned in them and put on to the fields to sweeten the acid soil in the north of the county. It was brought by small coasting ships, the anthracite coal coming from Hook or Saundersfoot and the limestone from the huge quarries of West Williamston.

Porth Clais and Caerbwdy had square ones, but mostly they were round; Solva, Porth Clais, Abereiddi, Porthgain, and Abercastle still have them. They were well built, probably because most were owned by the Bishop of St. Davids and it is good that they have been restored.

Holy Wells

These were probably originally a reflection of the old Celtic pre-Christian worship of water, and became curing wells. The Church found no difficulty in transferring their efficacy to the Church. In next to no time, they were adopted by one or other holy man.

St. Non's is, fortunately through its restoration, in the best of condition, much better than Pistyll Dewi where St. David was baptised at Porth Clais or that other Pistyll Dewi which St. David prayed for and which immediately flowed, running at times with wine and milk. It ran into the River Alun, sadly Sir G. G. Scott blocked it up in 1866. That great authority, Major Francis Jones, listed 18 different St. Davids wells, so space precludes a mention of them.

Chapels

Similarly, the chapels of the peninsula are well worth more than a mention. These vary between the majestic Wesleyan chapel in the city, so prominent that some people take it for the cathedral, to the small chapels built fifteen hundred or more years ago by the sea-faring holy men or peregrini who wanted a place to give thanks to God for a safe arrival through the dangerous waters round the coast. St. Justinians is a prototype of these, restored though it has been.

Vernacular Buildings

Pembrokeshire had a wonderful heritage of vernacular houses: tower houses, fortified houses, hall-houses, round-chimneyed farmhouses and cottages.

It would have been nice to say where some could be seen. Sadly, it is not possible, most are altered or covered with undergrowth.

True, some fine historical specimens remain, but mostly they are to be found under a mass of brambles or ivy, rotting away. If they were birds or scenery, there would have been a lobby, working hard to save them.

You should be able to see plenty of two-room cottages; mostly nowadays done up as holiday cottages. And there are plenty of 18C farmhouses still in situ.

But there is one type of farmhouse in the St. Davids area which should not be forgotten. These are the round-chimneyed houses, solid medium size farm-houses. When first described, they were thought to be mostly in the south of the county; then a dozen or so were described round the turn of the century in the St. Davids area; but it seems likely they were once really to be found over the whole county.

They all had what were called 'Flemish' chimneys, large inelegant round stone chimneys. Most probably they were a hangover from Norman castle builders. These houses had chimneys on the side of the house; and had extensions beyond the main walls called lateral outshuts. In the St. Davids area they have been destroyed or altered. The best-known remaining one is Rhosson, near St. Justinians. But probably the best example is that illustrated, which the authors restored and farmed for some years. This is in the Welsh-speaking Gwaun Valley, the furthest north one of this type has been found. It is still private.

If you want to see round, you'll have to go up to the Lake District where the National Trust has a fine one.

Beaches

Solva: Picturesque, long fjord-like harbour with boats. Beyond the Gribin, the headland to the east, is the pebbly sandy beach of the Gwadn. Sand at Solva itself but only when the tide is right out.

Porth y Rhaw: Small cove, a mile west of Solva.

Caerbwdy: Small bay south-east of St. Davids. A little sand at low water, but mainly shingle. Unspoilt and attractive.

Caerfai: Medium sized sandy beach, west of Caerbwdy. A favourite with children, firm sand, chocolate coloured rocks, rock pools. The road to it in St. Davids is signposted. A flight of steps and a steep track lead down.

Porthclais: A narrow sandy creek, nearly empty at low water. At the mouth of the River Alun a mile south-east from the city. Originally the port for St. Davids. Boats kept here. Car parking, in what was originally the gas works, limited. Not a bathing beach at all but good as a starting place for walks, or for a picnic.

Porthlysgi: Small shingle beach, covered at high water. Remote; access only on foot by Coast Path. No car parking anywhere near.

Porthstinian (St. Justinian's): Rocky cove, landing place for Ramsey Island. Lifeboat housed here. Not a good bathing beach, but fine for a picnic or as a starting point for cliff walk. Small car parks a few yards back. May be developed.

Porthsele: Small sandy cove adjoining Whitesands. Sand and rocks, most attractive, and not too crowded as a rule. Access normally by footpath either from Pencarnan or by Coast Path; on foot from Whitesands at low water.

Whitesands Bay (Porth Mawr): The finest beach in the north. A long stretch of firm sand. Fine surfing; toilets, refreshments, large car park (charge) right by the beach. Crowded in summer, but plenty of room at the ends. Swimming is safest south of the access road because of currents. Golf links just inland. No dogs.

Porth Melgan: Small, attractive, unspoilt cove nestling under St. Davids Head. Sandy, good swimming, but be careful of currents. Access limited to footpath only, from Coast Path, and nowhere nearer than Whitesands to park a car.

Beaches going north from Whitesands:

Aberpwll: Small cove a mile and half west of Abereiddi. Access only along Coast Path or by footpath from Pwllcaerog farm. No parking.

Abereiddi: A good sized beach reached off the coast road, the main impression is from the black stones, slate and shale. Fine beach, good walking either way. Parking.

Traethllyfn: A quite large, beach, between Porthgain and Abereiddi. High cliffs with steep steps down. Footpath access from Porthgain or Abereiddi or drive through Barry Island farm and park at the cliff top.

Porthgain: A tiny, sandy beach beside a picturesque little harbour, itself overshadowed by the immense derelict shell of the former stone – crushing plant. Parking. Pub, restaurant.

Aberfelin: Beach for Trefin. Small, shingly cove, very attractive.

Abercastle: Small, picturesque with harbour on the coast road between Trefin and Mathry. Limited parking.

Ancient Monuments

Archaeology tells us what people left behind them. Sadly, it does not always tell us the other things about them that we would like to know. But they certainly left a lot in the St. Davids area.

The earliest were the Neolithic stone age people, the earliest agriculturalists. Their large stone burial chambers, usually communal, date from 4000 B.C.

Here, on St. Davids Head, are a couple of small Neolithic tombs, and one larger one; and at Clegyr Boia, the rare dwelling house, or what was left of one. Up at Abercastle there is a very fine large cromlech, or megalithic tomb.

Although the next people, of the Bronze Age, left much in Wessex particularly, here their remains have been mainly small burial chambers and frequent Standing Stones.

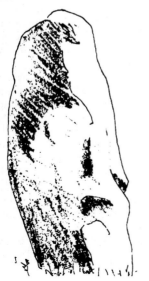

 A few of the latter have been excavated and in addition to being simple markers are sometimes part of larger complexes with ritual significance.

Intriguing, but irritating because nobody has any idea of what it means is Maen Dewi, a large standing stone by Rhodiad near St. Davids. And another is Rhos y Clegyrn up at St. Nicholas – if you are going up to Tregwynt Woollen Mill, go a bit further on.

The next people, the Celts, left their remains, in the shape of promontory forts all down the coasts, some of them very large indeed. And hundreds of fortified dwellings inland.

You can see the promontory forts at Castell Heinif, south of St. Justinians; at Penpleidiau between Caerfai and Caerbwdy, at Caerau between St. Davids and Abereiddy, at Porth y Rhaw by Solva and the Gribin at Solva, at Castell Coch up by Longhouse Farm and another Castell Coch by Penmorfa and biggest of all Garn Fawr up by Strumble Head.

Most intriguing of all is at St. Davids Head itself: Clawdd y Milwr, the Warrior's Dyke is drystone walling cutting off the headland with eight circular huts inside. Lots of material excavated from here now in Tenby Museum.

The rocky outcrop on the way to St. Justinians, Clegyr Boia, has a history covering all ages, being a neolithic dwelling, an Iron Age camp and the home of Boia himself, the enemy of St. David.

Folktales and Legends

The most interesting folk tales are those of the distant past, before Nonconformity and universal education eroded the belief in the Fair Folk.

First and probably the most ancient is taken from the Mabinogion, that ancient collection of medieval Welsh tales.

King Arthur and Kilhwch and Olwen

It is set in a very early medieval Pembrokeshire; just about when Saint David was active.

Kilhwch, son of a prince, fell in love with Olwen, daughter of the savage giant, Yspaddaden Penkawr.

"Go to Arthur your cousin," said his father, "and ask him to cut your hair and help you."

King Arthur offered the help of all his knights and they set out to achieve the seemingly impossible tasks set by the giant.

They had to grub up a hill, plough, sow and ripen the grain in a day, find the missing Mabon lost in infancy, hunt the Twrch Trwyth and perform numerous other tasks, and if successful, the giant would die.

Mabon was found by asking the oldest creatures, blackbird, stag, eagle, owl and salmon, the other tasks accomplished by magical help and the hunt for Twrch Trwyth begins.

The mysterious Twrch Trwyth was a monstrous boar, with seven young pigs, transformed for his sins from a King into a swine.

Between his ears he had a comb, razor and scissors which Arthur had to take as one of the impossible tasks.

So Arthur went to Ireland to ask for the comb etc., but the Twrch was so angry at being transformed to a swine that he wouldn't speak to Arthur, let alone yield comb, razor and scissors. What was more, he took the battle into Arthur's country. With his seven young pigs, he landed at Porth Clais. Arthur and his men, horses and dogs went to Mynyw (St. Davids), missing Twrch whom he overtook after the pigs had killed all they found of men and beasts along Aberdaugleddyf (Milford Haven).

Arthur followed Twrch Trwyth as far as Preseli and Twrch made a stand along the Nevern. From there he went to Cwm Cerwyn and slew four of Arthur's champions; and made a second stand and slew four more, and was wounded himself. The next morning before day, he killed four more and, with these, many men of the country.

Then Arthur pursued him to around Llandissilio and he killed four more before going on up to Cardiganshire; all over South Wales they chased the boar and pigs, losing many men. Eventually only Twrch himself was left and, in the Severn estuary, they seized the scissors and razor but he escaped to Cornwall where they managed to get the comb. But Twrch swam out to sea and was seen no more.

Kilhwch and Arthur's men went to the giant and cut off his head and Olwen became Kilhwch's wife.

The Green Isles of the Sea or Islands of Enchantment

A century ago, so the tradition says, sailors on the coast of Pembrokeshire had actually landed on islands out at sea where the Plant Rhys Ddwfn, Children of Rhys the Deep, lived. This was the name given in West Wales to the Fair Folk. The curious thing was that when the sailors returned to their boats, the islands simply vanished from view.

But the Fair Folk were well known: they used to come to local markets regularly at Haverfordwest, Milford, Laugharne, Cardigan and Fishguard. They were seen sometimes by a few sharp-sighted people, but their presence was known by many.

"Oh, they were here today," people used to say to each other on their way back from market when prices had been high and everything sold. Without speaking they bought their meat, corn and other necessities, putting down silver pennies as if knowing what they would have been charged. The farmers liked them because they bought corn well, but the poorer labourers resented their forcing up prices.

Gruffydd ab Einon was in St. Davids churchyard one day when he suddenly saw the islands out at sea. He went to put out to sea at once but the islands had disappeared; a second time, too, the same thing occurred. The third time, though, he took with him the turf on which he had been standing, and he landed on the islands safely. He was warmly welcomed by the little people and shown their many treasures, for they were great traders.

"How do you manage to stay here in safety?" he asked one little old man, before leaving.

"There are strange herbs that grow here and nowhere else, so that the islands cannot be seen. Only here do they grow and on the turf in St. Davids churchyard."

"But how can you be sure that one of you won't betray the secret of the herbs?" persisted Gruffydd.

"Oh," said the little man, "that is due to the teaching of Rhys. He told us to honour ancestors; to love our wives without looking at those of our neighbours and to do our best for our children. We do that, and no-one is unfaithful to another. A traitor is a wholly imaginary character among us: we see him with a head like the Devil, and ass's feet, and hands like a man's, holding a large knife and the family dead around him."

St. David & The Corpse Candle

The Corpse Candle was a light like that of a candle which was supposed to come from a house when a death was likely to occur.

It would then take the course of the funeral procession to the burial place. It was a pale bluish light moving slowly along a short distance above the ground.

Sometimes people see a resemblance to a skull carrying the candle; others would see the person who was to die carrying the candle.

There is a tradition that St. David himself prayed for a sign to the livng of the reality of another world. Originally it was confined to the St. Davids area.

In the sixth century, Saintship was already a profession in Wales, especially in the west and north. The Saints were, in many cases, itinerant monks coming from princely families. They sailed round the dangerous and rocky west and north coasts and founded their tiny cells, living simply and preaching their austere gospel, sometimes individually or sometimes in a community.

Nothing was recorded of their activities for hundreds of years, and when their biographies were written, the credulity of medieval religiosity revealed some strange things.

Heads were cut off, picked up and put back. Among others St. Winifred, St. Justinian, St. Cynog and St. Decumen suffered in this way. St. Piran sailed from Ireland on a sea monster, St. Feock on a granite boulder, and St. Decumen, as well as his headless accomplishment, sailed on a bundle of twigs. St. Brendan, riding from Ireland on a sea monster, met St. Barre riding the opposite way on a horse.

The austere St. David confined his miracles on the whole to occurrences of a religious nature – healing his teacher Paulinus's blindness, or raising a hill at Llandewi Brefi on which to preach against Pelagianism.

Language of the Fair Folk

There is only one reported case of an identified language spoken by the Fair Folk. Many of the fairy wives and Mermaids were reported as having spoken in Welsh.

This is the story Elidorus, or Elidyr, a priest, told the Bishop of St. Davids as reported by Giraldus in his Itinerary through Wales. When Elidorus was a boy of 12 he ran away from school to avoid the strict discipline and frequent canings. He hid in a river bank where he found a hollow; after a couple of days he was getting pretty hungry and wondering what to do about it, when two little men came up to him and invited him to a country 'full of delights and sports'. He followed them with alacrity through a dark path and then out into a most attractive countryside with rivers, meadows, woods and fields.

He was taken to a king who questioned him at length and then handed him over to his son, who was about the same age as Elidorus. They played together, and Elidorus learned quite a bit of the language.

He often went back to his own world; sometimes by the way he had first come, and sometimes by a different way.

He described the little people to his mother at great length. They were very small, he said, but well built, with fair complexion and long hair over their shoulders like women. They had small horses and greyhounds. They lived on a milk diet, made up 'into messes' with saffron, but they ate no meat or fish. They never took an oath and detested lies. They had no form of public worship, being devoted only to truth and each time they came back from our upper world, presumably from the markets, they couldn't stop talking about our infidelities, inconstancy and ambition.

But Elidorus's mother spoilt it by getting him to bring back one of the golden balls they used to play with; sadly two little men followed him and siezed it back again. Later in life, Elidorus told the story to David , Bishop of St. Davids.

He had learned quite a lot of the language of the little people and, according to the Bishop, it conformed in many ways to the Greek language, some words being identical, notably those for salt and water.

If, says Giraldus Cambrensis, a scrupulous enquirer should ask my opinion, I answer with Augustine "that the divine miracles are to be admired, not discussed."

What to do in Fine Weather

Here are a few suggestions about what to do in fine weather (and on the next page, what to do in less fine weather).

Firstly: **See the city**. That won't take very long, though shopping will spin it out a bit. But do that in indifferent weather.

Secondly: **See the Cathedral complex**. Good weather for this, because half the fun is walking round the Close and Bishop's Palace, which is out of doors.

Beaches: lots, big and small. If you have a car, north Pembrokeshire is open to you; and south down to Newgale and beyond. See page 25, and note parking arrangements. The bus service south is on the coast but north it is mainly a little inland.

Walking: the Coast Path round St. Davids is as good as anything you could want. Further afield: see our *Coast Path Guide* and *Best Walks in Pembrokeshire*.

Farm Park on the way to Whitesands. Rare breeds, 120 acres of beautiful scenery.

Ancient Monuments: This will take you to splendid scenery. The Neolithic builders had an eye for good burial sites.

Adventure holidays at Twr y Felin: leave the children for the day in the former windmill and hotel.

Places the Folktales relate to: it would be fun to track down the location of the folktales. Fine scenery, but don't try and find where Elidorus was taken. Giraldus Cambrensis doesn't give it.

Churches: the county has some nice ones. There is a rough division into Welsh types and English types. Llanhowel is one of the former; the latter are on the whole in the south of the county. Few are original, i.e. they have been rebuilt or extensively restored mostly last century. But so many are in the countryside.

Lifeboat: if it's not busy, go and have a look; at St. Justinians.

Castles: none round St. Davids worth bothering about. Roch is nearest and is private. Newport indifferent and not yet visitable. Fine ones further afield: Pembroke; Manorbier; Carew; Llawhaden and Lamphey; Cilgerran. And Picton, which is still lived in, only Sunday and Thursday: but there are also fine gardens, craft shop, restaurant in the courtyard.

Further is Carreg Cennen near Llandeilo. But very rewarding. Also has a rare breeds farm. If you go that far, then try Llansteffan. Then you might as well go to the **Boat House** at **Laugharne**, Dylan Thomas's house, on the way back.

There's always **Oakwood**, by Canaston Bridge.

Boat Trips to and round the Islands: Ramsey of course, Skomer too.

Swimming Pool and Tennis Courts in Secondary School. **Golf:** on the way to Whitesands.

Garden: with unusual plants in St. Davids.

Check with Information Centres for latest information.

What to do in Wet Weather

If, by any chance, it doesn't look too bright, don't despair. It's rarely bad for long.

First: **the Cathedral itself**. Then **shopping**: in St. Davids it is surprisingly good for so small a place. Bit short on antique shops – there are few in the whole county.

Craft shops etc., woollen shops in St. Davids, Fishguard, Trefin, Solva; other places too, but those are the nearest.

Woollen Mills: Tregwynt between St. Davids and Fishguard, sign-posted to the left just past Mathry – to the right is a sign-post for **Llangloffan Cheese-making farm**, demonstrations in the mornings. The other woollen mill is at Middle Mill, Solva. Try going there along the old road out of St. Davids: just past the County School, a little road forks left. It is a fine little road ending up at Middle Mill, very narrow and it exposes the disgraceful last war airfield, what's left of it. Ignore the new buildings.

Potteries: There's a potter at Caerfarchell, off the Fishguard road. The new Gallery in the High Street has some pots and so of course do the craft shops. The next nearest potter is at Solva and another at Little Haven; if you are going towards the centre of the county, try Wolfscastle.

Art Galleries: John Rogers and Stan Rosenthal in St. Davids and John Knapp-Fisher at Croesgoch, the longest established probably. At Porthgain there is both Alun Davies's art gallery and Harbour Lights gallery.

If you venture as far as Castle-martin, there are the Giardellis. But close at hand there are artists in Nun Street, and New Street and Peter Daniels' Pink Gallery at Nine Wells. Galleries too at Hendre Cross, Landeloy, at Pelcomb and Caerfarchell; and Fishguard.

Museums: Several small local museums though you'll have to travel. Scolton Manor, which also has large grounds, Penrhos Cottage at Llanycefn (appointment only), Tenby Museum includes paintings by Gwen and Augustus John; and interesting bits and pieces found on St. Davids Head. There is the tapestry of the last invasion of Britain at Fishguard, Pembrokeshire Motor Museum at Keeston, and museums at Narberth and Pembroke.

Woodworkers: at Mathry is Jim Harries' shop; and at Eweston.

Mills: If you're going down Haverfordwest way, go on to Blackpool Mill or on to Carew Mill.

The Sea: If you can't go to sea, see what the sea contains. St. Davids has its Oceanarium and Marine Life Centre.

Music: Probably more good music in St. Davids than anywhere else in the County. At the end of May there's a Festival. Other concerts as announced. Ask at the Bookshop. Also about Drama.

Any weather: call in at the Book Shop on the Pebbles.

Maps

The maps in this booklet are free-hand sketch maps; but they try to show relevant places.

For driving around the whole county, you will need the 1¼" O.S. maps 157, 158 and 145. For St. Davids alone 157 is adequate, but it stops short of Newport and the Preseli Hills; and it cuts the Gwaun Valley in half; so if you're opting to drive up there, and it's certainly worth it, you'll need O.S. 145, Cardigan.

And for Tenby and the Angle/Castlemartin area you'll need O.S. 158.

Perhaps you could make do with Bartholomew's No. 11, Pembroke and Carmarthen 1:100,000. It is certainly all right for driving, though for walking you need the O.S. 1:50,000 already mentioned or even the 1:250,000, the old 2½" to 1 mile.

If you are simply walking the Coast Path round St. Davids, you don't *need* any maps other than the ones contained in the booklet. St. Davids lies at the centre of the peninsula. It is only a shortish walk to any of the access points.

This applies to all parts of the coast we are talking about. There is good car parking at all of them. We have left out the long, handsome stretch from St. Davids Head to Trepwll by Abereiddi because there is not a good parking place.

*　　*　　*

Parking

Car parking is good in St. Davids.

There are several parking places in the city. If you are coming from Haverfordwest, there is the National Park Car Park, on the left. A charge is made.

If you are simply visiting the Cathedral there is a car park at the level of the Cathedral. Go down Goat Street, left hand corner of Cross Square. Charge.

Also for the Cathedral is Quickwell Hill car park, and there is one further car park in Nun Street. Charge.

Bibliography

Leaflets on the Bishop's Palace by the Dean; and on St. David and the Misericords by N. Rees are good.

I don't know what's come over publishers, all the best books, even modern ones, are out of print. For what's it worth, here they are:

> *Companion Guide to South Wales* by P. Howell and E. Beazley.
> *St Davids and Dewisland* by D. W. James.
> *Twr y Felin Guide to St Davids* by H. Evans.

Try and get copies.

Rhigyfarch's *Life of St David*; Giraldus Cambrensis' *Itinerary and Description of Wales* available in Penguin.